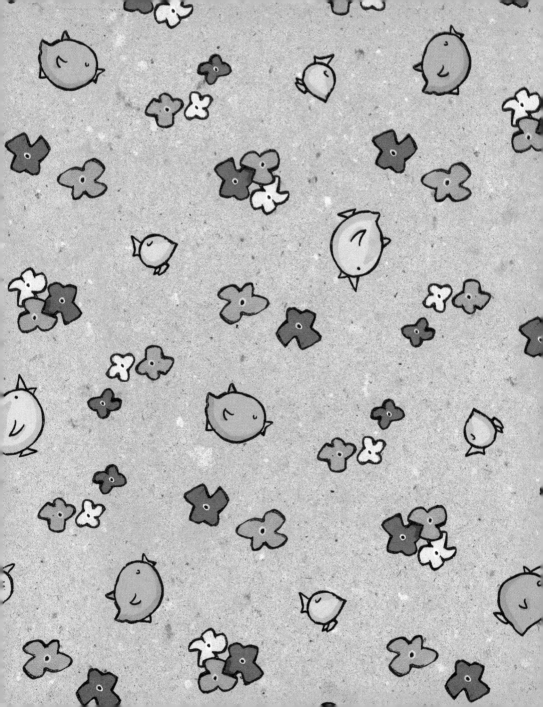

THANK YOU PRAYER

Adapted by Josephine Page

Illustrated by Caroline Jayne Church

SCHOLASTIC INC. Cartwheel B·O·O·K·S·®

New York   Toronto   London   Auckland   Sydney
Mexico City   New Delhi   Hong Kong   Buenos Aires

ISBN-13: 978-0-439-90174-1
ISBN-10: 0-439-90174-X

12 11 10 9 8 7 6 5 4 3 2   6 7 8 9 10 11/0

Printed in the U.S.A.   23

First Scholastic paperback printing, November 2006

For Ryan Alden Deas
— J.P.

For Oonagh, Natalie, and Freddie
— C.J.C.

Thank you for the food we eat.

Thank you for
the world so sweet.

Thank you for

the birds that sing.

Thank you, God, for everything.

Thank you
for my family.

Thank you, God,
for loving me.

For each and
every child, I pray...

And thank you for
this special day.

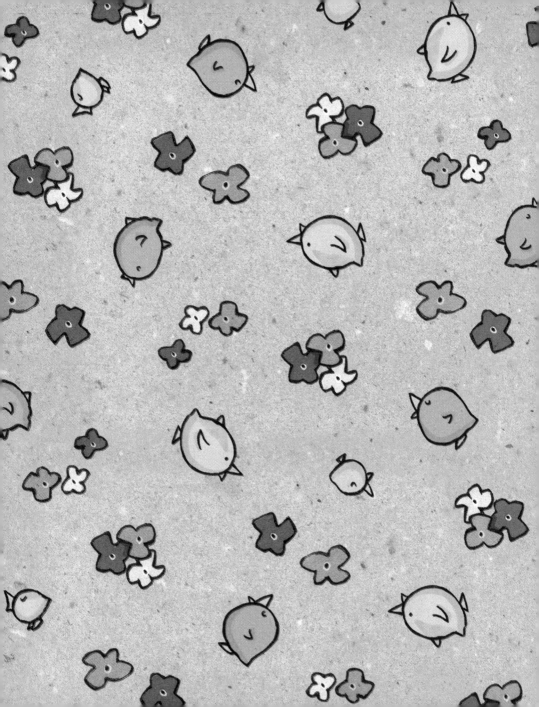